MEDICINE & ILLNESS

by

Grace Jones

Published in Canada
Crabtree Publishing
616 Welland Avenue
St. Catharines, ON
L2M 5V6

Published in the United States
Crabtree Publishing
PMB 59051
350 Fifth Ave, 59th Floor
New York, NY 10118

Published in 2019 by Crabtree Publishing Company

Author: Grace Jones

Editors: John Wood, Janine Deschenes

Design: Daniel Scase

Proofreader: Ellen Rodger

Production coordinator and prepress technician (interior): Margaret Amy Salter

Prepress technician (covers): Ken Wright

Print coordinator: Katharine Berti

Photographs
Front Cover – Zapp2Photo, TonyV3112. 2 – Photographee.eu 4 – Ljupco Smokovski, wavebreakmedia. 5 – VonaUA, Aila Images. 6 – Elnur, Phoenixns. 7 – Monkey Business Images, Alexander Raths, koh sze kiat. 8 – nobeastsofierce, bbernard. 9 – wavebreakmedia, Kateryna Kon. 10 – Ermolaev Alexander, Everett - Art. 11 – MAHATHIR MOHD YASIN, Margoe Edwards. 12 – Monkey Business Images. 13 – pathdoc, Photographee.eu. 14 – S_L, Csaba Deli. 15 – Rob Marmion, file404. 16 – Monkey Business Images, Tyler Olson. 17 – Diego Cervo. 18 – blvdone, public domaine / Wikimedia Commons. 19 – A3pfamily, fotovapl. 20 – frantab, SpeedKingz. 21 – life-literacy, anetta, st-fotograf. 22 – WeStudio, Kasa1982, Sherry Yates Young. 23 – Rob Byron, Pressmaster. 24 – By Master Video. 25 – sirtravelalot, Guzsudio. 27 – laranik. 28 – SUWIT NGAOKAEW. 29 – aceshot1. 30 – Monkey Business Images.

Printed in the U.S.A./082018/CG20180601

Library and Archives Canada Cataloguing in Publication

Jones, Grace, 1990-, author
Medicine and illness / Grace Jones.

(Our values)
Includes index.
Issued in print and electronic formats.
ISBN 978-0-7787-5190-8 (hardcover).--
ISBN 978-0-7787-5201-1 (softcover).--
ISBN 978-1-4271-2140-0 (HTML)

1. Medical anthropology--Juvenile literature. 2. Social medicine--Juvenile literature. I. Title.

GN296.J66 2018 j306.4'61 C2018-902415-1
C2018-902416-X

Library of Congress Cataloging-in-Publication Data

Names: Jones, Grace, 1990- author.
Title: Medicine and illness / Grace Jones.
Description: New York, New York : Crabtree Publishing Company, 2019. | Series: Our Values | Includes index.
Identifiers: LCCN 2018021339 (print) | LCCN 2018022028 (ebook) | ISBN 9781427121400 (Electronic) | ISBN 9780778751908 (hardcover) | ISBN 9780778752011 (pbk.)
Subjects: LCSH: Medicine--Juvenile literature. | Diseases--Juvenile literature.
Classification: LCC R130.5 (ebook) | LCC R130.5 .J66 2019 (print) | DDC 610--dc23
LC record available at https://lccn.loc.gov/2018021339

CONTENTS

Words that are **boldfaced** can be found in the glossary on page 31.

WHAT IS MEDICINE AND ILLNESS?

WHAT IS ILLNESS?

An illness is a sickness or a **disease** that affects our bodies and our minds. Illnesses can be short-term, lasting for a day or two, or long-term, lasting for years or even a lifetime. They can be serious and minor, or less serious. Minor illnesses, such as sore throats and colds, can usually be treated at home. Serious illnesses may require people to see a doctor or go to the hospital for treatment.

We can become ill for many different reasons. Some illnesses are caused by **pathogens** or living organisms, such as **bacteria** and viruses. Other illnesses are caused by our bodies not working properly. This might cause the body to attack itself. There are also illnesses which affect our minds, and how we think and feel.

WHAT IS MEDICINE?

The practice of **diagnosing, preventing,** or treating an illness is called medicine. Medicine is also what we call the drugs that we take to treat our illnesses. For example, sometimes a doctor might diagnose us with an illness and **prescribe** drugs which will make us feel better again. There are many different types of medicines that can treat thousands of different illnesses. Medicine can be used to take away pain and to manage diseases. Medicine can also cure diseases. It takes a lot of time, money, and reseraech to develop medicines that can cure diseases.

In our society, we experience and encounter different kinds of illness every day. We may become ill ourselves, know someone who is ill, or see illness represented in the media we consume. As a society, we also rely on medicine and other health care to treat us when we are ill and keep us healthy. This book helps you learn about the different illnesses and medicines in our world, the ways that health care professionals work to keep us healthy, and new innovations in the medical field.

TYPES OF ILLNESS

There are many different types of illness. Most illnesses are common and can be easily treated. However, sometimes an illness is much more serious. Without the proper medicine, a serious illness might even be life-threatening. Characteristics about you, such as your age, health, and **lifestyle choices**, can affect how your body responds to an illness.

A fever means your body temperature is too high.

THE COMMON COLD

Less serious illnesses can normally be diagnosed and treated by a doctor or nurse at a doctor's office. Illnesses like these can include common colds, sore throats, and minor **infections**. Usually these illnesses are treated with medicine, and a few days of rest.

Allergies are caused by the body reacting to harmless things, called allergens, as if they were a pathogen. Many allergies are not serious and can be treated by a doctor. However, allergies can be life-threatening. If a person with a serious allergy comes into contact with the allergen, they may experience **anaphylaxis**, which can cause death. When this happens, they need to quickly go to hospital for treatment.

PETS, POLLEN, AND FOOD SUCH AS NUTS ARE COMMON CAUSES OF ALLERGIC REACTIONS.

MENTAL ILLNESS

Some illnesses are difficult to see because they affect a person's mental health rather than their physical health. Mental illnesses are health conditions that involve changes in emotion, thinking, or behavior. Mental illnesses can be difficult to diagnose, and many people do not realize that they are suffering from a mental illness for a long time. It is important to talk about mental health and our emotions so we can understand how we feel and not keep it hidden away. It is not known exactly what causes most mental illnesses, but it can be affected by genes, day-to-day life, or differences in the brain.

Social anxiety, obsessive compulsive disorder (OCD), and personality disorders are all examples of mental illnesses. OCD is an anxiety disorder in which people have uncontrollable, repeated thoughts which they can't ignore. These thoughts may be unhelpful or unwanted.

DEPRESSION IS A MENTAL ILLNESS THAT CAUSES A PERSON TO FEEL EXTREME SADNESS, NUMBNESS, TIREDNESS, OR HOPELESSNESS. PEOPLE WHO HAVE DEPRESSION OFTEN FIND IT DIFFICULT TO COMPLETE EVERYDAY TASKS, SUCH AS EATING AND BATHING.

Mental illnesses are usually treated with psychotherapy, or talk therapy. This treatment involves regular counseling with a therapist, **social worker**, or **psychologist**. The patient voices their thoughts and feelings to their counselor who tries to understand why they feel the way they do and how to create strategies to help them feel better.

GENETIC DISEASES

Some diseases can be caused by a change in a person's genes. If a person is born with abnormal genes, or genes that are different from regular genes, their body may not work properly. Genes are the units of DNA that allow parents to pass on characteristics to their children. Gene abnormalities are called genetic diseases or disorders.

These are what a person's genes might look like under a very strong microscope.

THERE ARE AROUND 20,000 GENES IN THE HUMAN BODY.

Genetic diseases usually affect a person their entire life, from the time they are born. Sometimes, genetic diseases can develop later in life. Some genetic diseases can be passed on from parent to child. It is possible for parents to pass on genetic diseases such as cystic fibrosis (see page 13). Other genetic dieases are not inherited from parents. They might come from environmental factors. It's also possible to inherit genes that make it more likely for a person to develop a genetic disease, such as heart disease.

CHRONIC ILLNESS

Chronic illnesses are long-term illnesses that progress, or build, gradually and do not have an easy treatment or cure. They are sometimes illnesses that last for a person's whole life. These illnesses can be treated with medicine, but not cured. Asthma is a chronic illness. This illness causes attacks in which the airways in a person's lungs restrict, making it hard to breathe. Asthma attacks can be treated with an inhaler, pictured below, which helps a person breathe in medicine. Diabetes is another chronic illness. It is a disease in which the body cannot produce or use insulin, a chemical that controls the amount of sugar in the blood. People who have diabetes must eat a special diet and sometimes take insulin injections to stay healthy.

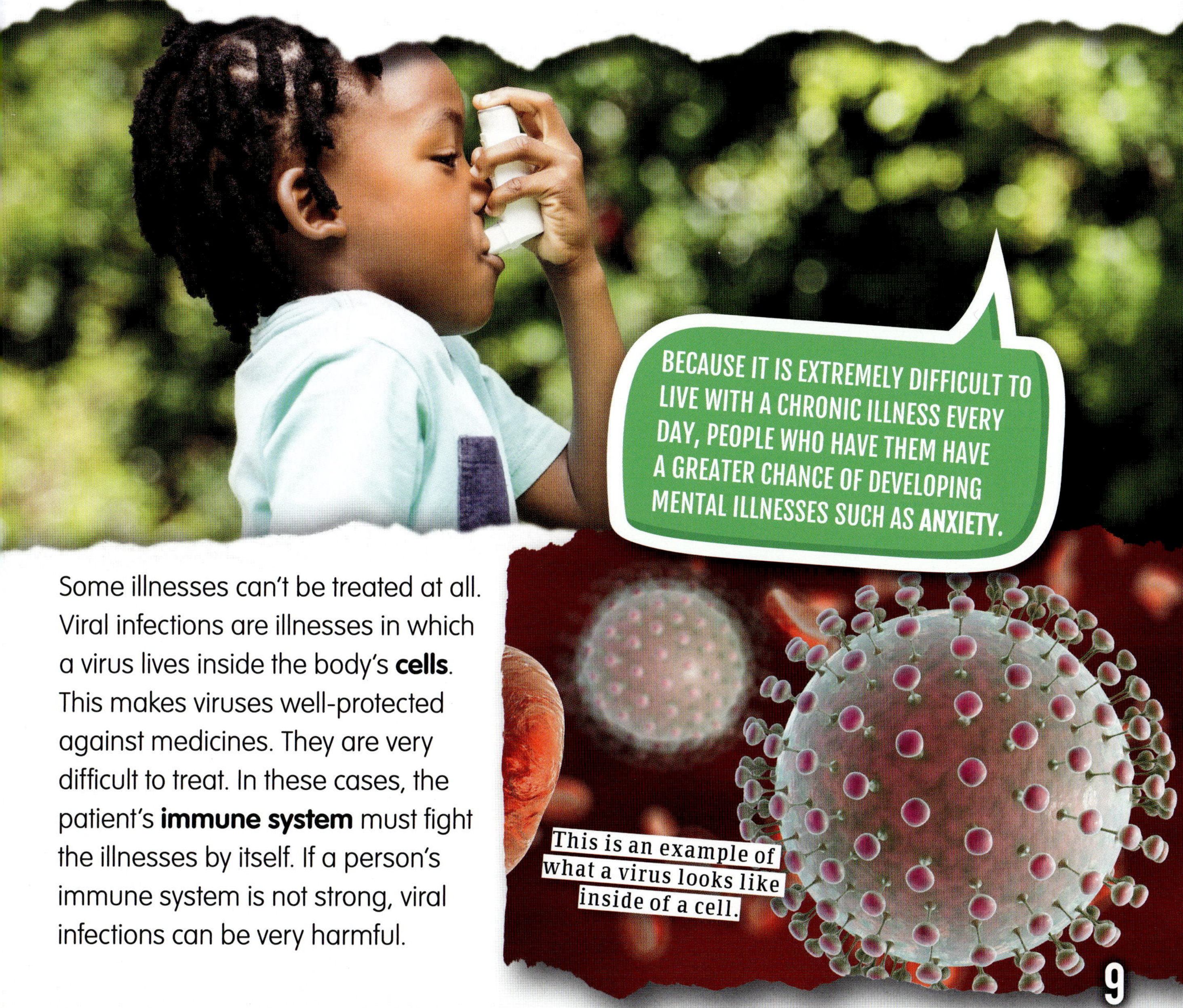

BECAUSE IT IS EXTREMELY DIFFICULT TO LIVE WITH A CHRONIC ILLNESS EVERY DAY, PEOPLE WHO HAVE THEM HAVE A GREATER CHANCE OF DEVELOPING MENTAL ILLNESSES SUCH AS **ANXIETY**.

Some illnesses can't be treated at all. Viral infections are illnesses in which a virus lives inside the body's **cells**. This makes viruses well-protected against medicines. They are very difficult to treat. In these cases, the patient's **immune system** must fight the illnesses by itself. If a person's immune system is not strong, viral infections can be very harmful.

This is an example of what a virus looks like inside of a cell.

CONTAGIOUS ILLNESSES

Some illnesses can spread from person to person. Others cannot be spread. Illnesses that spread between people, such as the flu and colds, are called contagious illnesses. They can spread in different ways. One way people can spread some illnesses is through physical contact. This can include touching an infected person or touching something that an infected person has touched. Another way contagious illnesses spread is through tiny organisms called microbes, also known as germs, in the air. When a person who has a contagious illness sneezes or coughs, they release the germs into the air, which then travel to others.

ONE WAY AN INFECTED PERSON CAN STOP THE SPREAD OF MICROBES IS TO COUGH OR SNEEZE INTO A TISSUE.

Doctors and scientists first realized that germs caused illnesses in the 1800s. Before then, people had many ideas and guesses about what caused illnesses. Many doctors thought a type of "bad air" made people ill. Some people thought diseases were caused by different amounts of fluid in the body, and others thought bad spirits were the cause.

Today, medicine is based on facts that have been tested again and again to make sure they are true. We now know that contagious diseases are caused by microbes and viruses, which are easily spread between people.

Some contagious illnesses cause serious problems when they spread to many people. An epidemic is when a contagious disease spreads within a large population of people very quickly. A pandemic is a global disease outbreak. Epidemics and pandemics be deadly when the diease spreads to areas of the world where health care is not available or not affordable. They can also be deadly when a person with a compromised, or unhealthy, immune system catches the diease.

IN SOME COUNTRIES IN ASIA, SUCH AS JAPAN, PEOPLE OFTEN WEAR MASKS TO PROTECT THEMSELVES FROM CONTAGIOUS ILLNESSES OR POLLUTION THAT CAN CAUSE ILLNESSES IN THE LUNGS.

You can do a number of things to protect yourself against catching contagious illnesses. Wash your hands regularly—especially before you eat. Clean surfaces, such as your desk at school, and areas you use often, such as your kitchen at home. Ask your parents or guardians about getting vaccinated. To be vaccinated means to recieve a substance called a vaccine that prevents you from contracting certain illnesses. If you have a contagious illness, try to avoid coming into close contact with others until you are better. Cough or sneeze into a tissue and wash your hands.

SERIOUS ILLNESSES

A serious illness is usually defined as being an illness that requires a person to receive regular medical treatment and spend time in the hospital. Also called critical illnesses, people usually have to take time off school or work to be treated for serious illnesses. They can be life threatening—but there are many treatments available to help people fight and recover from serious illnesses.

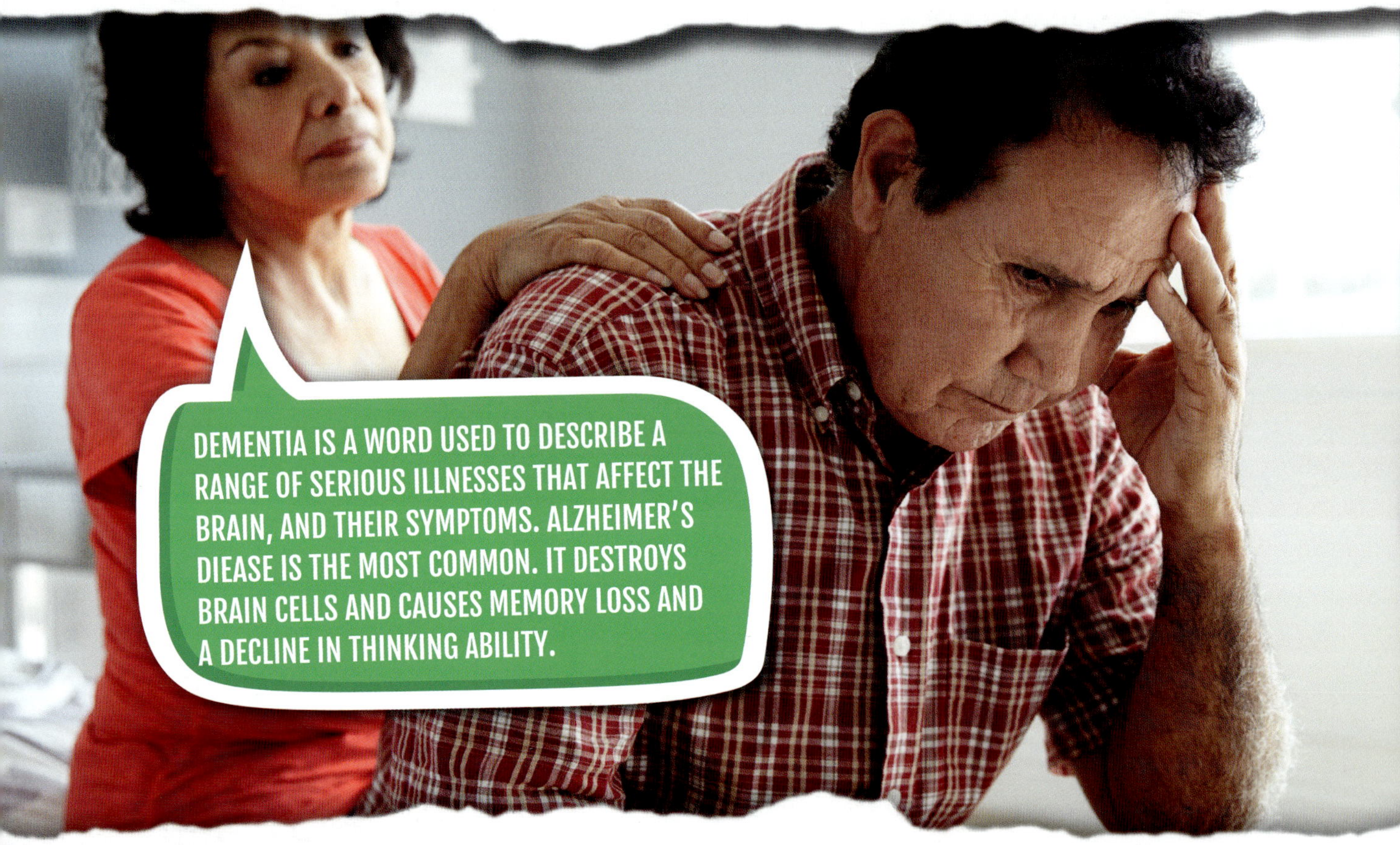

DEMENTIA IS A WORD USED TO DESCRIBE A RANGE OF SERIOUS ILLNESSES THAT AFFECT THE BRAIN, AND THEIR SYMPTOMS. ALZHEIMER'S DIEASE IS THE MOST COMMON. IT DESTROYS BRAIN CELLS AND CAUSES MEMORY LOSS AND A DECLINE IN THINKING ABILITY.

CANCER

Cancer is a disease that causes a cell in the body to become abnormal. This cell grows and multiplies into a growth called a tumor. There are many different types of cancer and they can affect many different parts of the body. Each type is different. There are many different ways to treat cancer as well, such as surgery to remove the tumor, **radiation** treatment, and **chemotherapy**. Ongoing research means new individualized treatments are emerging each year. Many cancers, especially those that are diagnosed early, can be successfully treated and in many cases, cured.

MENINGITIS

Meningitis is a very serious illness that affects the **membranes** around the brain and spinal cord. There are many different types of meningitis. Viral meningitis is the most common. It is not usually life-threatening and usually involves flu-like symptoms. Bacterial meningitis can be very serious and those who recover can be left with permanent **disabilities**, such as hearing loss or brain damage. However, as long as it is treated as soon as possible, most people recover from the illness.

COMMON SYMPTOMS OF BACTERIAL MENINGITIS INCLUDE A HIGH FEVER, VOMITING, HEADACHES, AND A STIFF NECK.

CYSTIC FIBROSIS

Cystic fibrosis is another serious illness. It is a genetic disorder which causes damage to the lungs and **digestive system**. People who have cystic fibrosis produce a lot of **mucus** that makes it difficult for them to breathe and digest food. They often get lung infections. There is currently no cure for cystic fibrosis, but it can be treated with medicine that helps the lungs fight infection and **physiotherapy** techniques that help clear mucus from the chest. Some patients even have lung transplants.

THIS CHILD WHO HAS CYSTIC FIBROSIS IS USING A MACHINE THAT DELIVERS MEDICINE TO HER LUNGS.

TREATING ILLNESSES

DIAGNOSIS

Usually the first step in treating an illness is diagnosing it. Depending on how serious the illness is, a patient visits a doctor's office or a hospital when they become ill. There, they are assessed by a doctor or nurse who can sometimes diagnose them there, or send them to another doctor who specializes, or focuses, in certain illnesses. To diagnose a patient, doctors might check their **heart rate**, listen to their breathing, or measure their **blood pressure**. Sometimes doctors take a blood or urine sample to be tested in a laboratory.

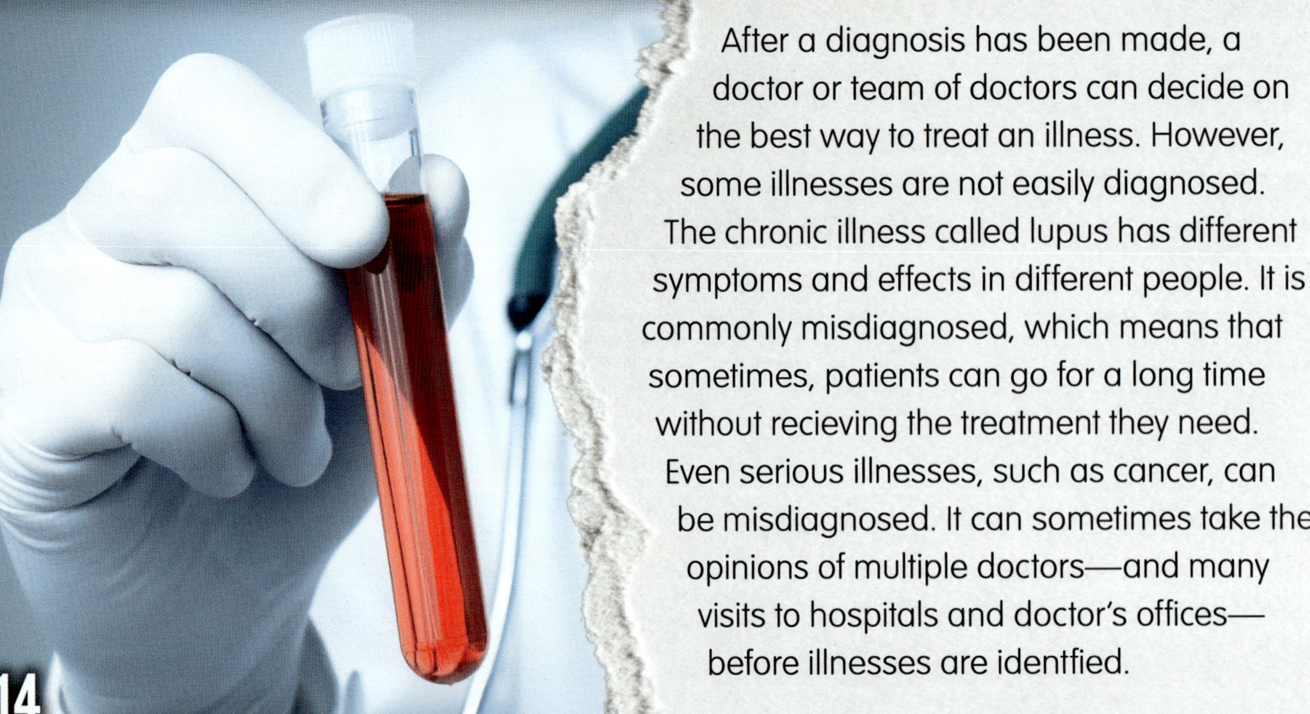

After a diagnosis has been made, a doctor or team of doctors can decide on the best way to treat an illness. However, some illnesses are not easily diagnosed. The chronic illness called lupus has different symptoms and effects in different people. It is commonly misdiagnosed, which means that sometimes, patients can go for a long time without recieving the treatment they need. Even serious illnesses, such as cancer, can be misdiagnosed. It can sometimes take the opinions of multiple doctors—and many visits to hospitals and doctor's offices—before illnesses are identfied.

ILLNESS PREVENTION

Most doctors agree that the best way to treat many common illnesses is to prevent them from happening in the first place. There are some illnesses we are born with or cannot prevent. But for many illnesses, there are lifestyle choices that we can make to decrease our chances of developing them.

We can avoid common colds and flus by eating healthy, exercising, and taking steps to avoid germs. We can avoid high-risk behaviors such as smoking and abusing alcohol. We can get vaccinated for many illnesses, such as the flu, chicken pox, whooping cough, and polio.

Everyday tasks, such as properly brushing and flossing our teeth, can help promote health and prevent illness.

HEART DISEASE IS AN EXAMPLE OF AN ILLNESS THAT CAN BE PREVENTED BY A HEALTHY DIET AND EXERCISE.

Some serious illnesses can be prevented with healthy lifestyle choices, too. For example, coronary heart disease is much more common in those who smoke, have an unhealthy diet, or are overweight. Coronary heart disease is when **plaque** builds up and thickens on the walls of a person's **arteries**. A person who exercises regularly and eats a healthy diet has a significantly lower risk of developing coronary heart disease.

TYPES OF TREATMENT

After somebody is diagnosed, they can receive treatment. For most minor and some chronic or serious illnesses, a doctor can prescribe medicine that will treat the illness. For example, antibiotics are a type of medicine that is used to treat infections caused by bacteria. Mental illnesses can sometimes be treated with medicine, but it often must be coupled with forms of talk or behavior therapy too.

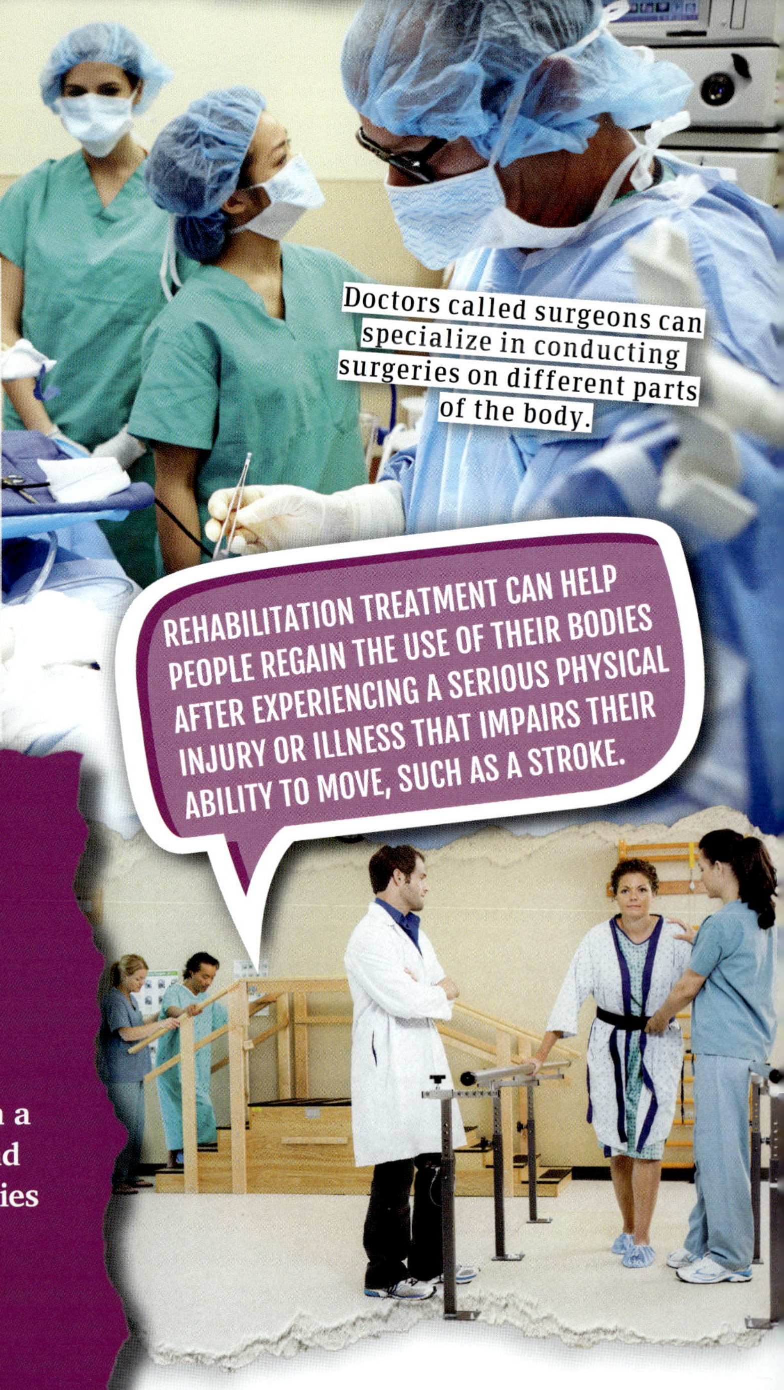

Sometimes, for more complicated or serious illnesses, surgery may be the only treatment option. Surgery is a type of treatment where doctors make **incisions** using special equipment to look inside and repair a part of the body. For example, if a patient has a cancerous tumor, a specialist doctor may decide to remove the tumor with surgery.

Doctors called surgeons can specialize in conducting surgeries on different parts of the body.

REHABILITATION TREATMENT CAN HELP PEOPLE REGAIN THE USE OF THEIR BODIES AFTER EXPERIENCING A SERIOUS PHYSICAL INJURY OR ILLNESS THAT IMPAIRS THEIR ABILITY TO MOVE, SUCH AS A STROKE.

Therapy is a type of treatment which uses exercises and changes in behavior to help people get better over a long time. Physiotherapy helps with physical problems, and involves special stretches and exercises to help the body heal. Psychotherapy, or counselling, helps support mental health and treat mental illness. It involves regular meetings with a professional to talk through thoughts and emotions, and develop plans and strategies to improve mental health by changing thoughts and behaviors.

LONG-TERM MANAGEMENT

If a patient's illness cannot be cured, treatment often involves long-term management of pain and other symptoms. Doctors treat the effects of an illness when they cannot treat the illness itself. They might prescribe painkillers to lessen pain, medication to help patients sleep, or medication that helps lower blood pressure.

For example, some people have a long-term illness called arthritis, which causes their joints to become stiff and painful. Doctors often prescribe painkillers to help alleviate their symptoms. Long-term management also involves having regular visits with a doctor to monitor the patient's health.

PALLIATIVE CARE CAN ALSO INCLUDE END-OF-LIFE CARE, WHICH GIVES SUPPORT AND CARE TO A PERSON NEARING THE END OF THEIR LIFE.

People who have serious long-term illnesses may receive palliative care. Palliative care is specialized medical care that focuses on providing relief from the symptoms of serious illnesses. The aim of palliative care is to improve the quality of life for the patients and their families.

People who receive palliative care may stay in a hospice, which is a type of hospital that provides treatment to people with very serious and often disabling illnesses. Hospices and palliative care also usually provides counselling support for a patient and their families.

TYPES OF MEDICINE

Medicines are used to treat, prevent or manage illnesses. They have been developed, updated, and improved in many ways over thousands of years.

Scientific research is an important part of medicine, and can lead to many new cures and treatments.

ANTIBIOTICS AND INFECTION

Antibiotics are prescribed to treat infections that are caused by bacteria. Most bacteria that live in the body are harmless. Some are even helpful, such as those found in the intestines that help us digest food. Antibiotics kill a harmful bacteria or stop it spreading around your body.

Alexander Fleming was a scientist who discovered the first antibiotic, penicillin, by accident in 1928. After growing some mold on a dish, he left his laboratory to go on vacation. When he came back, he found that the mold had killed all the bacteria around it. He and many other scientists did more research, which has led to the wide range of antibiotics which we use today.

ALEXANDER FLEMING

VACCINATIONS

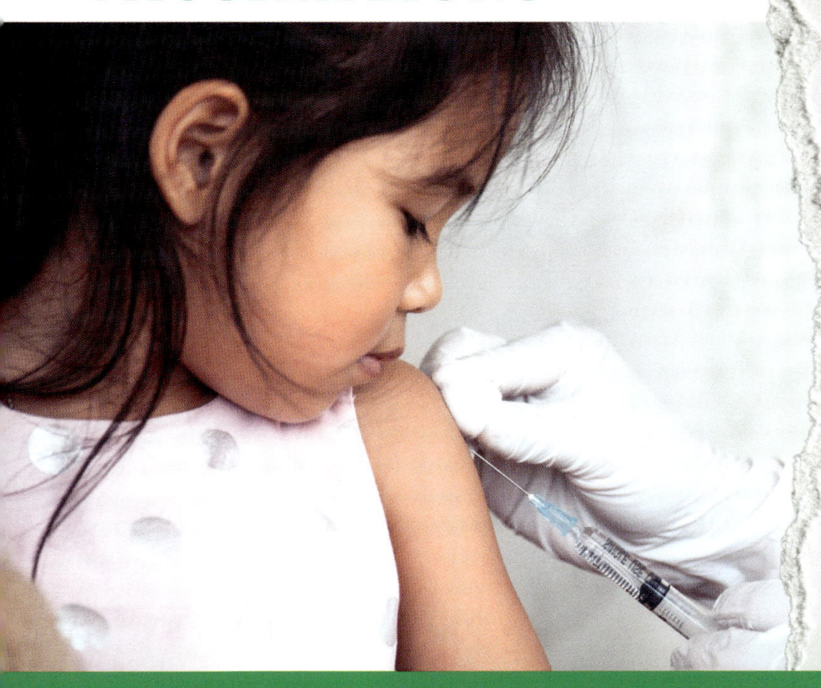

Vaccinations are given to people to prevent them from getting a disease in the future. A vaccination is an injection of a very weak form of a disease. After the injection, the body fights the weak form of the illness. Once the body has learned how to fight the disease, it will be able to fight the stronger forms. People who have had vaccinations are **immune** if they come into contact with certain types of diseases later in life.

In the 1700s, Edward Jenner was the first person to create a successful vaccine. He gave a disease called cowpox to a boy, which made him immune to the much deadlier disease of smallpox. In the 1800s, biologist Louis Pasteur studied how vaccines worked, and discovered more vaccines for serious diseases, such as rabies. Since then, millions of lives have been saved through the use of vaccines. Today, we use vaccines to protect us from many illnesses, such as polio, tuberculosis, and measles. Before vaccines, these diseases killed many children. It is important to be vaccinated as a first defense against these diseases.

VACCINES ARE USUALLY GIVEN AT A YOUNG AGE TO MAKE SURE CHILDREN DON'T CONTRACT DISEASES THEY WILL BE UNABLE TO FIGHT—DUE TO THEIR LESS-DEVELOPED IMMUNE SYSTEMS.

TREATMENT FOR CANCER

A number of treatments are used for cancer. The treatment used depends on the type of concer. Patient may have surgery to remove cancerous tumors. Doctors may also use radiation treatment. Radiation treatment works by damaging and killing the cancer cells using high-energy radiation. Sometimes the radiation is produced by a piece of material that is put inside the body, and sometimes the radiation is produced by a machine outside the body. Chemotherapy is another common treatment for cancer. This includes a drugs that stop or slow the growth of cancer cells. New treatments for cancer are developed every year. Some now involve triggering an immune response from the body or using **stem cells** to kill cancer cells.

CHEMOTHERAPY HAS A NUMBER OF DIFFICULT SIDE EFFECTS. IT CAN CAUSE A PERSON TO FEEL EXTREMELY SICK AND TIRED. IT CAN ALSO CAUSE A PATIENT TO LOSE THEIR HAIR.

MEDICINE FOR MENTAL HEALTH

Aside from therapy, mental illnesses may also be treated with some types of medicine. The medicines vary widely, but most work to help regulate a person's emotions and thoughts. These may not fully treat the problem, but can help to manage it while the patient receives different types of support. It can sometimes be challenging for doctors to find medicines that work to treat mental heath, because every person's brain is unique to them.

Doctors are working to find ways to more quickly diagnose and effectively treat mental illnesses.

ANTIHISTAMINES

People who suffer from some allergies, such as seasonal allergies to certain plants or allergies to animals, might take medicines called antihistamines. Antihistamines work by blocking the body's allergic responses. This stops symptoms such as a runny nose, watery eyes, and itchy skin. Because allergies are reactions to harmless substances, antihistamines don't need to treat the illness, just the symptoms.

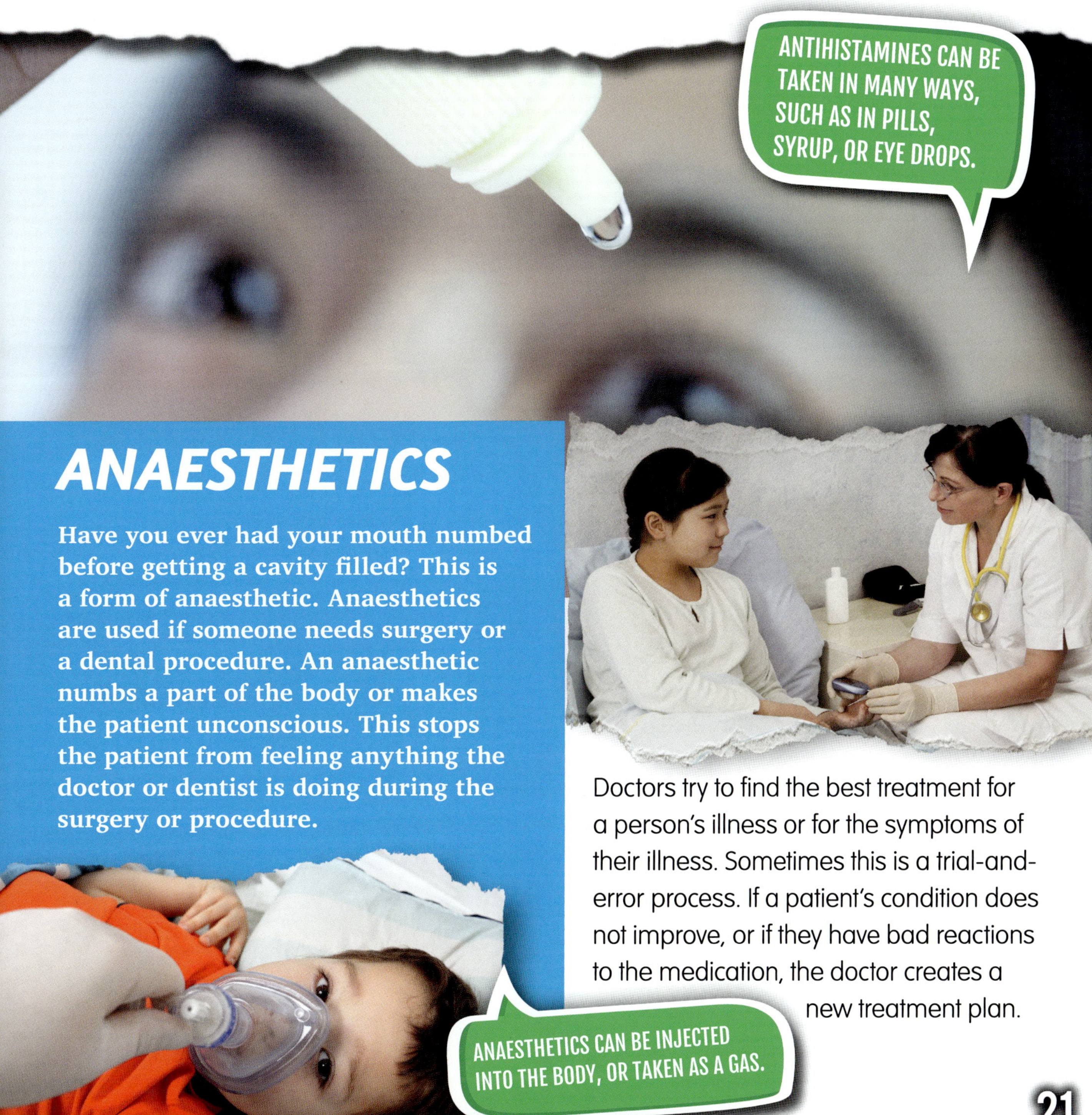

ANAESTHETICS

Have you ever had your mouth numbed before getting a cavity filled? This is a form of anaesthetic. Anaesthetics are used if someone needs surgery or a dental procedure. An anaesthetic numbs a part of the body or makes the patient unconscious. This stops the patient from feeling anything the doctor or dentist is doing during the surgery or procedure.

Doctors try to find the best treatment for a person's illness or for the symptoms of their illness. Sometimes this is a trial-and-error process. If a patient's condition does not improve, or if they have bad reactions to the medication, the doctor creates a new treatment plan.

MEDICAL EQUIPMENT

DOCTORS AND NURSES

Doctors, nurses, and other professionals often use special equipment to assess a patient and treat them. In a doctor's office, a doctor may use a stethoscope to listen to the heartbeat or breathing of a patient. They may also use an ophthalmoscope, which shines a light into the eye to check if it is working correctly. Doctors also use scales to weigh patients, an otoscope to look into a patient's ears, a thermometer to check a patient's body temperature, and a blood pressure cuff to measure blood pressure.

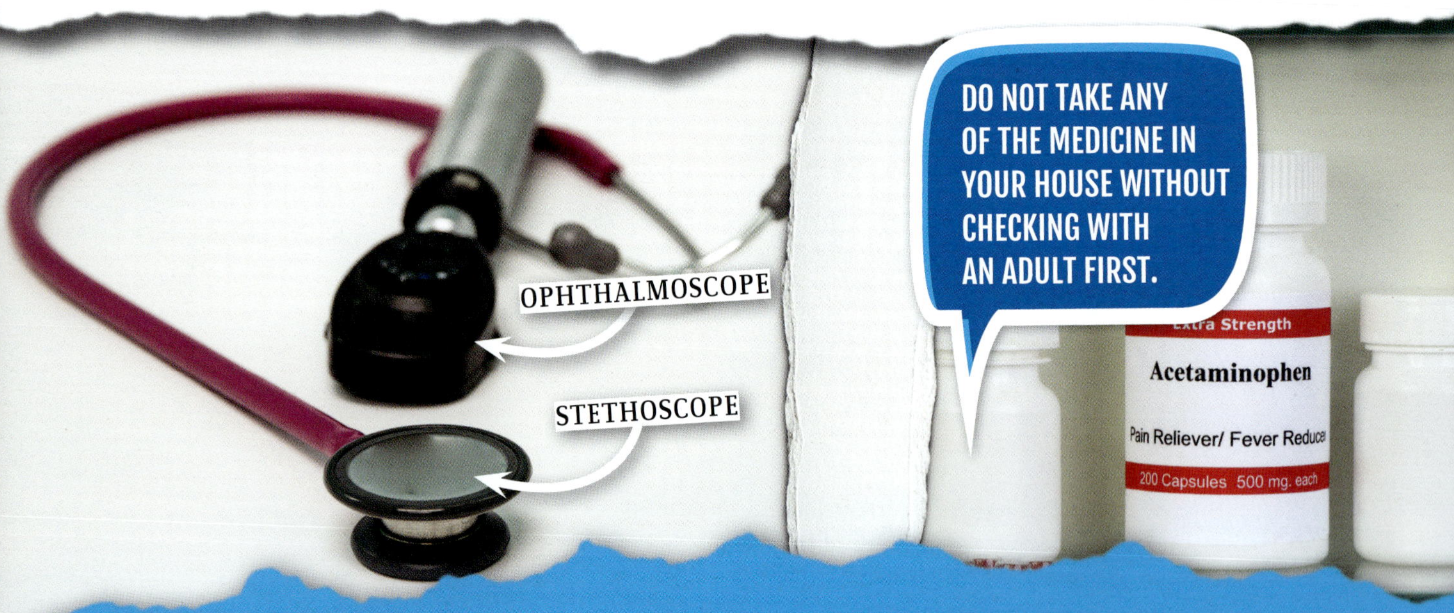

There is probably medical equipment in your home, too. When you feel ill, your parents or guardians may use a thermometer to check your body temperature. A high temperature may mean that you have a fever or the flu. You probably also have medicine at home—both prescriptions for you and your family members, or over-the-counter medicine you can buy without a prescription. Some examples of over-the-counter medicine include acetaminophen pills to relieve headache pain, cough medicine to relieve coughing, and antacid medicines to relieve stomach pain.

If someone has a long-term illness or condition, they might have special equipment that they need to carry around with them. For example, if someone has asthma, they carry their inhalers everywhere in case they have an asthma attack. If someone has an illness which makes it hard to move around, they may need a mobility device such as a wheelchair, a scooter, or a walker.

HOSPITAL EQUIPMENT

In hospitals, healthcare professions use a variety of machines and equipment to treat people. Doctors may use an X-ray machine or an MRI machine to take scans of the inside of your body. This allows doctors to look at your bones, teeth, and tissue to see if there is a problem inside the body. Doctors and nurses may use needles or an IV drip to administer medicine in a person's body. Doctors and nurses may also track information such as a person's blood pressure and heart beat on a monitor. During surgery, surgeons use a range of specialized tools, too.

INNOVATIONS IN MEDICAL EQUIPMENT

Medical equipment is the tools that allow a healthcare professional to do their job. From robotic surgery to advanced prosthetics, the tools that are used by doctors evolve along with medicine.

Even young innovators around the world are working to create medical tools that will make it easier for healthcare professionals to diagnose, treat, and prevent illnesses.

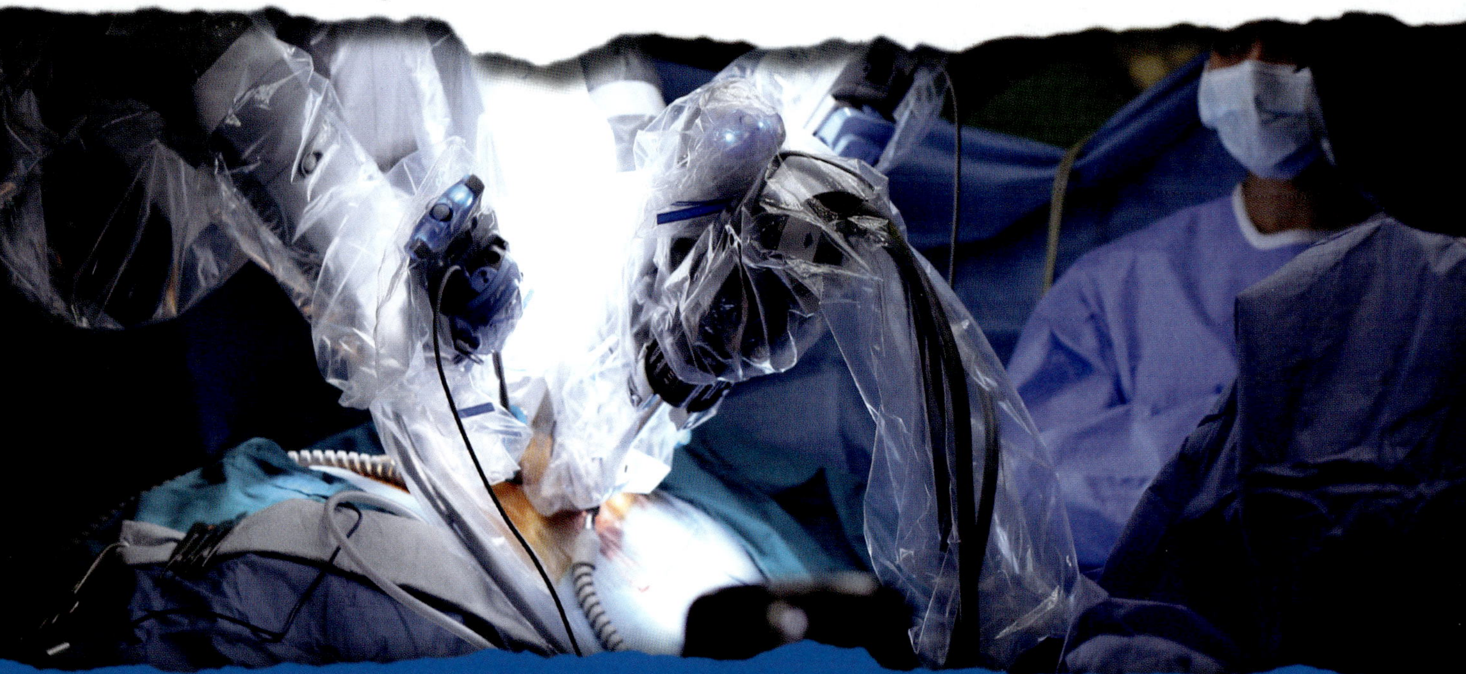

ROBOTIC SURGERY

Innovations in robotics have allowed surgeons to save lives in ways that were not possible in the past. Robots can perform more delicate and complex surgery than humans are able to, because they allow for higher control and precision and can help doctors work on hard-to-access parts of the body. Using robotic machines in surgery can also sometimes mean that the surgery is less invasive. This means that because of a robot's precision, smaller cuts are made into the body. A widely-used robotic surgery system includes robotic arms with surgical tools and a camera that gives a close-up view of the work. They are controlled by a surgeon who watches his work through the camera. Some surgeries in which robots are used include those on the heart, kidneys, and colon.

MODERN PROSTHETICS

Prosthetics are devices that can replace body parts. Millions of people worldwide wear them to replace lost limbs—usually arms, legs, hands, and joints. Innovations in prosthetics are ongoing, and mean that the once uncomfortable and stiff prosthetics now act in a very similar way to our limbs. Most prosthetics are now lightweight, comfortable, and high-performance. Wearing them, people can do most daily activities, and even extreme ones, such as mountain biking. Research is even being done with sensors that could allow people to use their sense of touch while wearing prosthetics.

IN ANURUDH'S HOMELAND OF INDIA, VACCINES CAN BE DIFFICULT TO ACCESS BECAUSE MANY PEOPLE LIVE IN SMALL, REMOTE VILLAGES WITH NO REFRIGERATION TO KEEP VACCINES COOL.

A YOUNG INNOVATOR

In 2015, 15-year-old Anurudh Ganesan invented Vaxxwagon, a tool that can deliver lifesaving vaccines to remote communities around the world. Vaccines must be kept cool to be effective. This means they cannot be transported to remote communities without refrigeration. Anurudh was inspired to create Vaxxwagon because of his own history. When he was a baby, his grandparents travelled ten miles to get him vaccinated—only for the vaccines to be too warm when they arrived. Vaxxwagon can transport vaccines by bicycle and keeps them cool using a pedal-powered refrigeration system.

UNIVERSAL ACCESS

According to the United Nations' **Universal Declaration of Human Rights** and the World Health Organization (WHO), health and well-being are **human rights**. This includes the right to access acceptable and affordable health care. Many people do not have access to the care they need because of a lack of care where they live, or because they cannot afford care. Others do not have access to acceptable care. Acceptable care benefits a person's health and is free from unfair treatment. According to the WHO, some **marginalized** groups of patients, such as transgender or disabled people, experiece human rights **violations** while being cared for.

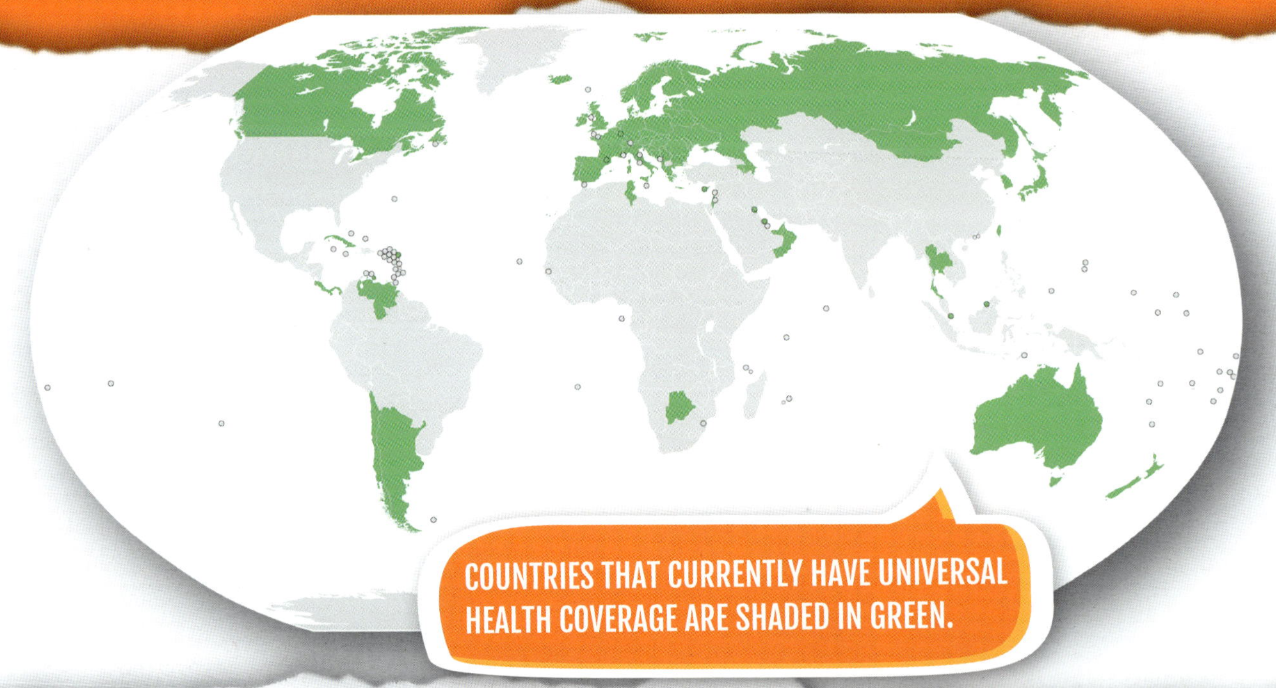

COUNTRIES THAT CURRENTLY HAVE UNIVERSAL HEALTH COVERAGE ARE SHADED IN GREEN.

UNIVERSAL HEALTH COVERAGE

Universal health coverage or healthcare is a system that makes sure all citizens of a country can access the healthcare they need without financial strain. It reflects the view that every person has the right to receive quality healthcare— regardless of their financial situation. Universal health coverage exists in countries such as Canada, Germany, Japan, Russia, and Sweden. It is often paid for by the government, which funds the care with money they collect as **taxes**. This means that everyone in the country looks after each other by paying a little bit towards a healthcare insurance system for all.

DOCTORS WITHOUT BORDERS

Achieving universal access to healthcare is a goal for many organizations around the world. One such organization is Médecins Sans Frontières, or Doctors Without Borders. It is dedicated to treating people who are not able to get the healthcare that they need. The treatment is free, and the doctors who are part of the organization travel all over the world to provide treatment. Doctors are often sent to countries where there are natural disasters, wars, or an outbreak of a serious disease. An important part of Doctors Without Borders is that they are neutral. This means they do not discriminate about who they provide treatment to. They do not choose sides in a war or conflict.

This is a ship which Doctors Without Borders uses to travel around the world.

In 1999, Doctors Without Borders won the Nobel Peace Prize for all the work that it has done. The organization has saved the lives of millions of people in more than 80 countries.

DOCTORS WITHOUT BORDERS IS A CHARITY WHICH PEOPLE CAN DONATE MONEY TO. DONATIONS HELP THE ORGANIZATION CARRY ON TREATING PEOPLE AROUND THE WORLD.

MEDICINE IN THE FUTURE

The development of medicine has already saved millions of lives. Medicine has changed and evolved throughout history and will continue to do so.

Scientists, researchers, and doctors are making discoveries every day that will help save millions of lives in the future.

SEARCHING FOR CURES

Right now, researchers around the world are working on developing new drugs and treatments for serious illnesses. Cures can involve effectively treating diseases, and also vaccines that prevent people from contracting diseases in the first place. Research is ongoing and can take a very long time, but people are not giving up. In the near future, we may have a way to cure diseases such as diabetes, the brain disease called Alzheimers, and heart disease. For example, research is being done on stem cells. These cells may be able to replace diseased cells in our body and repair damage.

ANTIBIOTICS

We rely on antibiotics as lifesaving tools against infections. However, they are becoming less effective. When exposed to antibiotics, some bacteria can become resistant to them. This means that the more we use antibiotics, the more bacteria will become antibiotic-resistant. Because of this, scientists must continue to make new antibiotics every year. There is worry that over time, antibiotic-resistant bacteria will be more common and make treating people for infections much more difficult. A lot of research needs to be done to ensure that this doesn't happen.

MANY PEOPLE TAKE PART IN CHARITY EVENTS TO HELP TO RAISE MONEY FOR MEDICAL RESEARCH, SUCH AS THIS RUN FOR BREAST CANCER IN OHIO.

SUPPORTING THE CAUSE

Doctors Without Borders is just one example of the huge number of charities that raise money for disease research, provide support to patients and their families, help give heathcare in communities that need it, and raise awareness about different illnesses. Other examples include Project C.U.R.E, which provides medical supplies and tools to communities in need, and World Cancer Research Fund International, which unites cancer charities. Ronald McDonald House also has programs to help children and provides family members with low-cost stays and meals when their children are in hospitals far from home.

THINK ABOUT IT

In what ways has medicine changed over the years? What are some innovations in the medical field that interest you? Discuss your ideas with your classmates.

Imagine that you are ill with a contagious illness. Write down some of the ways that you could stop the illness from spreading to others.

Discuss your thoughts about whether heathcare is a human right. Do you think that every country should have universal healthcare for its citizens? Why or why not?

GLOSSARY

allergies A sensitive reaction of the body to an outside substance

anaphylaxis A serious allergic response to a substance that can be fatal if not treated

anxiety A mental illness in which a person has extreme feelings of worry and nervousness

arteries Vessels that carry blood from the heart to other parts of the body

bacteria Living organisms found everywhere on Earth. Bacteria can be helpful or cause harm.

blood pressure A measure of the force of blood against the walls of the blood vessels

cells The smallest unit of all living things

chemotherapy The use of chemicals to treat a disease—especially to treat cancer

colon Part of the large intestine

diagnosing Identifying an illness or problem based on symptoms

digestive system The system in the body through which nutrients from food are absorbed and waste is dispelled

disabilities A condition that limits a person's physical or mental abilities

disease A condition that causes a disorder in how the body functions

heart rate The number of heartbeats in a specified time period, such as one minute

human rights Rights, or things people are allowed to have or do, that all people should have because they are human

immune Free from or not susceptible to

immune system The system that protects the body from foreign substances

incisions Cuts, especially during surgery

infections The invasion of the body by disease-causing organisms

laboratory A room with scientific equipment used for research or teaching

lifestyle choices Decisions that influence the way a person lives.

marginalized Treating a person or group as lesser than

membranes A barrier or thin layer between units or structures in the body

mental health A person's psychological wellbeing

mucus Thick liquid produced in the body

pathogens Disease-causing bacteria, viruses, or microorganisms

physiotherapist A professional who treats physical ailments through physical methods such as stretching and massaging

plaque Build-up of a fatty substance on the walls of the arteries

prescribe Recommend and allow the use of a medicine or treatment

preventing Stopping something from happening

psychologist A professional who studies and treats the human mind, emotions, and behavior

radiation Energy in the form of waves; radiation therapy involves emitting waves to kill diseased cells in the body

resistant Opposing or withstanding something

social worker A professional who provides assistance to those in need

stem cells Unspecialized cells in the body that can become any kind of specialized cell

taxes Monetary contributions to a government, usually by money taken off one's income

Universal Declaration of Human Rights A document adopted by the United Nations in 1948 that outlines the basic human rights that every person on Earth should have

violations Failures to respect a person's rights

INDEX